The
Poetry of
Emily
Dickinson

The
Poetry of
Emily
Dickinson

SIRIUS

SIRIUS

This edition published in 2020 by Sirius Publishing, a division of
Arcturus Publishing Limited,
26/27 Bickels Yard, 151–153 Bermondsey Street,
London SE1 3HA

ISBN: 978-1-78888-470-9
AD006631US

Printed in China

Contents

Introduction

Barely published in her own lifetime, in death Emily Dickinson achieved a posthumous fame unparalleled in American literary history. But for her sister, Lavinia, it is doubtful that her poems would ever have been printed. However, when the first volume was published four years after her death, it met with stunning success, going through eleven editions in less than two years.

Emily was born in Amherst, Massachusetts, in December 1830. The Dickinsons' house, the Homestead on Main Street, was the center of Amherst society. The young Emily was a brilliant student with great social flair. She was full of gaiety and wit, and regularly "rode out" with suitors, though nothing came of these attachments.

In an era of religious revivals, Emily's interests were firmly set towards science and nature. In 1847, she attended Mount Holyoke Female Seminary, an establishment with a strong tradition of evangelical Christianity. Years later, a fellow student, Clara Turner, recalled the moment when the headmistress "asked all those who wanted to be Christians to rise." Emily remained seated. No one else did. Turner reports Emily's comment to her: "'They thought it queer I didn't rise' – adding with a twinkle in her eye, 'I thought a lie would be queerer.'"

With her formal education at an end, Emily should have taken up the social niceties of her station, including daily rounds of visits. But she refused, instead baking bread, gardening, or writing letters. She was a vigorous letter writer, some scholars speculating that this was a kind of "visiting without distraction."

In 1856, her brother Austin married a close friend of Emily's, Susan Gilbert, and the couple built a house next door called the Evergreens. This small family enclave was perfect for the retiring Emily and inspired the start of a creative streak. By the age of 36, she had written more than a thousand poems, many of them copied out in small, self-made booklets and stored in her writing desk. Her poems were widely read by her friends and correspondents—Susan Gilbert received over 200 poems in letters from Emily—but hardly ever published.

Scholars have long been intrigued by the sudden creative outpouring, giving rise to a "before and after" theory set around an invisible catastrophe or "terror" that Emily referred to in some of her letters, possibly a failed romantic liaison or a nervous illness. However, recent evidence suggests that she suffered from epilepsy, a condition which existed in the family and one that in those days was usually dealt with in private.

Whatever prompted it, at this point Emily's poems had a new-found confidence. Her unique style was simple, to the point, and expressive. Many take on the cadence and rhythm of hymns with four-beat and three-beat lines. Using light, almost jaunty, language, they address lofty themes with great power: the soul, love, rebellion, freedom, salvation, escape, and death, her sweet tone often masking deep meaning and intense emotion. That these subjects should be so shrewdly observed by a reclusive, birdlike spinster speaks volumes about the character of someone who had the courage to reject God.

In 1862, she sent examples of her work to Thomas Higginson in response to an article in *Atlantic Monthly*. A well-known literary figure, Higginson was not exactly effusive in his praise of her work and, in turn, she took little notice of his advice, but they began a correspondence that would last for the rest of Emily's life.

In the mid-1860s, Emily suffered eye problems, staying with relations in Boston while undergoing treatment. She returned home in late 1865 and rarely ventured again beyond the grounds of the Homestead until her death, 20 years later, of Bright's disease, in 1886.

Shortly after Emily's death, Lavinia found a cache of some 1,700 poems and hundreds of letters. She gave the material to Mabel Todd, who became increasingly enthusiastic about the beauty and power of the poems she read. With the help and encouragement of Thomas Higginson, the first edition of these poems was published in 1890. They received extraordinary praise from leading magazines and newspapers. The *New York Times* claimed Emily Dickinson would soon be among the immortals of English-speaking poets. That they were not wrong is borne out by this beautifully illustrated collection, which includes some of her finest and most significant works, such as "A bird came down the walk," "Wild Nights — Wild Nights!," "'Hope' is the thing with feathers," and "Because I could not stop for Death."

Even today, the bold voice of her poems can't be categorized: "I'm Nobody," says Emily, "— who are you?" Hers is a voice that can't be ignored, confrontational, even invasive, with a piercing question about our being.

There is another sky
Ever serene and fair,
And there is another sunshine,
Though it be darkness there —
Never mind faded forests, Austin,
Never mind silent fields —
Here is a little forest
Whose leaf is ever green —
Here is a brighter garden —
Where not a frost has been,
In its unfading flowers
I hear the bright bee hum,
Prithee, my Brother,
Into my garden come!

Awake ye muses nine, sing me a strain divine,
Unwind the solemn twine, and tie my Valentine!

Oh the Earth was made for lovers, for damsel, and hope-
less swain,
For sighing, and gentle whispering, and unity made of
twain.
All things do go a courting, in earth, or sea, or air,
God hath made nothing single but thee in His world so
fair!
The bride, and then the bridegroom, the two, and then the one,
Adam, and Eve, his consort, the moon, and then the sun;
The life doth prove the precept, who obey shall happy be,
Who will not serve the sovereign, be hanged on fatal
tree.
The high do seek the lowly, the great do seek the small,
None cannot find who seeketh, on this terrestrial ball;
The bee doth court the flower, the flower his suit receives,
And they make merry wedding, whose guests are
hundred leaves;
The wind doth woo the branches, the branches they are
won,
And the father fond demandeth the maiden for his son.
The storm doth walk the seashore humming a mournful
tune,
The wave with eye so pensive, looketh to see the moon,
Their spirits meet together, they make their solemn vows,
No more he singeth mournful, her sadness she doth lose.
The worm doth woo the mortal, death claims a living
bride,
Night unto day is married, morn unto eventide;

Earth is a merry damsel, and *heaven* a knight so true,
And Earth is quite coquettish, and beseemeth in vain to
  sue.
Now to the *application*, to the reading of the roll,
To bringing thee to justice, and marshalling thy soul:
Thou art a *human* solo, a being cold, and lone,
Wilt have no kind companion, thou *reap'st* what thou hast
  sown.
Hast never silent hours, and minutes all too long,
And a deal of sad reflection, and *wailing* instead of song?
There's *Sarah*, and *Eliza*, and *Emeline* so fair,
And *Harriet*, and *Susan*, and she with curling hair!
Thine eyes are sadly blinded, but yet thou mayest see
Six true, and comely maidens sitting upon the tree;
Approach that tree with caution, then up it boldly climb,
And seize the one thou lovest, nor care for *space*, or *time*!
Then bear her to the greenwood, and build for her a
  bower,
And give her what she asketh, jewel, or bird, or flower
  —

And bring the fife, and trumpet, and beat upon the
  drum —
And bid the world Goodmorrow, and go to glory home!

"Sic transit gloria mundi"
"How doth the busy bee"
"Dum vivamus vivamus"
I stay mine enemy! —

Oh "veni vidi vici!"
Oh caput cap-a-pie!
And oh "memento mori"
When I am far from thee!

Hurrah for Peter Parley!
Hurrrah for Daniel Boone!
Three cheers, sir, for the gentleman
Who first observed the moon —

Peter put up the sunshine!
Pattie arrange the stars
Tell Luna, tea is waiting
And call your brother Mars!

Put down the apple, Adam,
And come away with me,
So shalt thou have a pippin
From off my Father's tree!

I climb the "Hill of Science"
I "view the Landscape o'er;"
Such transcendental prospect
I ne'er beheld before!

Unto the Legislature
My country bids me go;
I'll take my india rubbers,
In case the wind should blow!

During my education,
It was announced to me
That gravitation stumbling,
Fell from an apple tree!

The Earth upon an axis
Was once supposed to turn,
By way of a gymnastic
In honor to the sun!

It was the brave Columbus,
A sailing o'er the tide,
Who notified the nations
Of where I would reside!

Mortality is fatal,
Gentility is fine,
Rascality, heroic,
Insolvency, sublime!

Our Fathers being weary,
Laid down on Bunker Hill,
And tho' full many a morning
Yet they are sleeping still!

The trumpet, sir, shall wake them,
In streams I see them rise,
Each with a solemn musket
A marching to the skies!

A coward will remain, Sir,
Until the fight is done;
But an immortal hero
Will take his hat, and run.

Good bye, Sir, I am going;
My country calleth me;
Allow me, Sir, at parting,
To wipe my weeping e'e.

In token of our friendship
Accept this "Bonnie Doon,"
And when the hand that pluck'd it
Hath passed beyond the moon,

The memory of my ashes
Will consolation be;
Then farewell Tuscarora,
And farewell, Sir, to thee!

On this wondrous sea
Sailing silently,
Ho! Pilot, ho!
Knowest thou the shore
Where no breakers roar,
Where the storm is o'er?

In the peaceful west
Many the sails at rest —
The anchors fast —
Thither I pilot thee!
Land Ho! Eternity!
Ashore at last!

I have a Bird in spring
Which for myself doth sing —
The spring decoys.
And as the summer nears —
And as the Rose appears,
Robin is gone.

Yet do I not repine
Knowing that Bird of mine
Though flown —
Learneth beyond the sea
Melody new for me
And will return.

Fast in a safer hand
Held in a truer Land
Are mine —
And though they now depart,
Tell I my doubting heart
They're thine.

In a serener Bright,
In a more golden light
I see
Each little doubt and fear,
Each little discord here
Removed.

Then will I not repine,
Knowing that Bird of mine
Though flown
Shall in distant tree
Bright melody for me
Return.

I haven't told my garden yet —
Lest that should conquer me.
I haven't quite the strength now
To break it to the Bee —

I will not name it in the street
For shops would stare at me —
That one so shy — so ignorant
Should have the face to die.

The hillsides must not know it —
Where I have rambled so —
Nor tell the loving forests
The day that I shall go —

Nor lisp it at the table —
Nor heedless by the way
Hint that within the Riddle
One will walk today —

I often passed the village
When going home from school —
And wondered what they did there —
And why it was so still —

I did not know the year then —
In which my call would come —
Earlier, by the Dial,
Than the rest have gone.

It's stiller than the sundown.
It's cooler than the dawn —
The Daisies dare to come here —
And birds can flutter down —

So when you are tired —
Or perplexed — or cold —
Trust the loving promise
Underneath the mould,
Cry "it's I," "take Dollie,"
And I will enfold!

Whose cheek is this?
What rosy face
Has lost a blush today?
I found her — "pleiad" — in the woods
And bore her safe away.

Robins, in the tradition
Did cover such with leaves,
But which the cheek —
And which the pall
My scrutiny deceives.

If she had been the Mistletoe
And I had been the Rose —
How gay upon your table
My velvet life to close —
Since I am of the Druid,
And she is of the dew —
I'll deck Tradition's buttonhole —
And send the Rose to you.

There's something quieter than sleep
Within this inner room!
It wears a sprig upon its breast —
And will not tell its name.

Some touch it, and some kiss it —
Some chafe its idle hand —
It has a simple gravity
I do not understand!

I would not weep if I were they —
How rude in one to sob!
Might scare the quiet fairy
Back to her native wood!

While simple-hearted neighbors
Chat of the "Early dead" —
We — prone to periphrasis
Remark that Birds have fled!

Heart! We will forget him!
You and I — tonight!
You may forget the warmth he gave —
I will forget the light!

When you have done, pray tell me
That I may straight begin!
Haste! lest while you're lagging
I remember him!

The rainbow never tells me
That gust and storm are by,
Yet is she more convincing
Than Philosophy.

My flowers turn from Forums —
Yet eloquent declare
What Cato couldn't prove me
Except the birds were here!

New feet within my garden go,
New fingers stir the sod;
A troubadour upon the elm
Betrays the solitude.

New children play upon the green,
New weary sleep below;
And still the pensive spring returns,
And still the punctual snow!

For every Bird a Nest —
Wherefore in timid quest
Some little Wren goes seeking round —

Wherefore when boughs are free —
Households in every tree —
Pilgrim be found?

Perhaps a home too high —
Ah Aristocracy!
The little Wren desires —

Perhaps of twig so fine —
Of twine e'en superfine,
Her pride aspires —

The Lark is not ashamed
To build upon the ground
Her modest house —

Yet who of all the throng
Dancing around the sun
Does so rejoice?

South Winds jostle them —
Bumblebees come —
Hover — hesitate —
Drink, and are gone —

Butterflies pause
On their passage Cashmere —
I — softly plucking,
Present them here!

Success is counted sweetest
By those who ne'er succeed.
To comprehend a nectar
Requires sorest need.

Not one of all the purple host
Who took the flag today
Can tell the definition,
So clear, of victory —

As he, defeated — dying —
On whose forbidden ear
The distant strains of triumph
Break, agonized and clear.

Safe in their Alabaster Chambers —
Untouched by Morning
And untouched by Noon —
Sleep the meek members of the Resurrection
    —

Rafter of satin,
And Roof of stone.

Light laughs the breeze
In her Castle above them —
Babbles the Bee in a stolid Ear,
Pipe the Sweet Birds in ignorant cadence —
Ah, what sagacity perished here!

Grand go the Years — in the crescent — above
    them —
Worlds scoop their arcs —
And firmaments row —
Diadems — drop — and Doges —
    surrender —
Soundless as dots — on a disk of snow —

Who never lost, are unprepared
A Coronet to find!
Who never thirsted
Flagons, and Cooling Tamarind!

Who never climbed the weary league —
Can such a foot explore
The purple territories
On Pizarro's shore?

How many Legions overcome —
The Emperor will say?
How many Colors taken
On Revolution Day?

How many Bullets bearest?
Hast Thou the Royal scar?
Angels! Write "Promoted"
On this Soldier's brow!

A science — so the Savants say,
"Comparative Anatomy" —
By which a single bone —
Is made a secret to unfold
Of some rare tenant of the mold,
Else perished in the stone —

So to the eye prospective led,
This meekest flower of the mead
Upon a winter's day,
Stands representative in gold
Of Rose and Lily, manifold,
And countless Butterfly!

The Daisy follows soft the Sun,
And when his golden walk is done,
　　Sits shyly at his feet.
He, waking, finds the flower near.
Wherefore, marauder, art thou here?
　　Because, sir, love is sweet!

We are the flower, Thou the Sun!
Forgive us, if as days decline,
　　We nearer steal to Thee, —
Enamoured of the parting West,
The peace, the flight, the Amethyst,
　　Night's possibility!

A fuzzy fellow, without feet,
Yet doth exceeding run!
Of velvet, is his Countenance,
And his Complexion, dun!

Sometime, he dwelleth in the grass!
Sometime, upon a bough,
From which he doth descend in plush
Upon the Passer-by!

All this in summer.
But when winds alarm the Forest Folk,
He taketh Damask Residence —
And struts in sewing silk!

Then, finer than a Lady,
Emerges in the spring!
A Feather on each shoulder!
You'd scarce recognize him!

By Men, yclept Caterpillar!
By me! But who am I,
To tell the pretty secret
Of the Butterfly!

A *Wounded* deer leaps highest,
I've heard the Hunter tell;
'T is but the ecstasy of *death*,
And then the Brake is still.

The *Smitten* rock that gushes,
The *trampled* Steel that springs:
A Cheek is always redder
Just where the Hectic stings!

Mirth is the Mail of Anguish,
In which it Cautions Arm,
Lest anybody spy the blood
And "You're hurt" exclaim!

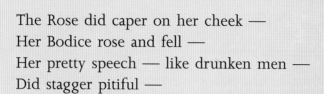

The Rose did caper on her cheek —
Her Bodice rose and fell —
Her pretty speech — like drunken men —
Did stagger pitiful —

Her fingers fumbled at her work —
Her needle would not go —
What ailed so smart a little Maid —
It puzzled me to know —

Till opposite — I spied a cheek
That bore *another* Rose —
Just opposite — Another speech
That like the Drunkard goes —

A Vest that like her Bodice, danced —
To the immortal tune —
Till those two troubled — little Clocks
Ticked softly into one.

"Faith" is a fine invention,
For Gentlemen who *see*!
But microscopes are prudent
In an Emergency!

I taste a liquor never brewed —
From tankards scooped in Pearl —
Not all the Vats upon the Rhine
Yield such an Alcohol!

Inebriate of Air — am I —
And Debauchee of Dew —
Reeling — thro endless summer days —
From inns of Molten Blue.

When "Landlords" turn the drunken Bee
Out of the Foxglove's door,
When Butterflies — renounce their "drams" —
I shall but drink the more!

Till Seraphs swing their snowy Hats —
And Saints — to windows run —
To see the little Tippler
Leaning against the — Sun —

A feather from the Whippoorwill
That everlasting — sings!
Whose galleries — are Sunrise —
Whose Opera — the Springs —
Whose Emerald Nest the Ages spin
Of mellow — murmuring thread —
Whose Beryl Egg, what Schoolboys hunt
In "Recess" — Overhead!

I shall know why, when Time is over,
And I have ceased to wonder why;
Christ will explain each separate anguish
In the fair schoolroom of the sky.

He will tell me what "Peter" promised,
And I, for wonder at his woe,
I shall forget the drop of Anguish
That scalds me now, that scalds me now!

My River runs to thee —
Blue Sea! Wilt welcome me?
My River waits reply —
Oh Sea — look graciously —
I'll fetch thee Brooks
From spotted nooks —
Say — Sea — Take Me!

Dying! Dying in the night!
Won't somebody bring the light
So I can see which way to go
Into the everlasting snow?

And "Jesus"! Where is Jesus gone?
They said that Jesus — always came —
Perhaps he doesn't know the House —
This way, Jesus, Let him pass!

Somebody run to the great gate
And see if Dollie's coming! Wait!
I hear her feet upon the stair!
Death won't hurt — now Dollie's here!

Musicians wrestle everywhere —
All day — among the crowded air
I hear the silver strife —
And — waking — long before the morn —
Such transport breaks upon the town
I think it that "New Life"!

It is not Bird — it has no nest —
Nor "Band" — in brass and scarlet — drest —
Nor Tamborin — nor Man —
It is not Hymn from pulpit read —
The "Morning Stars" the Treble led
On Time's first Afternoon!

Some — say — it is "the Spheres" — at play!
Some say that bright Majority
Of vanished Dames — and Men!
Some — think it service in the place
Where we — with late — celestial face —
Please God — shall Ascertain!

A slash of Blue —
A sweep of Gray —
Some scarlet patches on the way,
Compose an Evening Sky —
A little purple — slipped between —
Some Ruby Trousers hurried on —
A Wave of Gold —
A Bank of Day —
This just makes out the Morning Sky.

Make me a picture of the sun —
So I can hang it in my room —
And make believe I'm getting warm
When others call it "Day"!

Draw me a Robin — on a stem —
So I am hearing him, I'll dream,
And when the Orchards stop their tune —
Put my pretense — away —

Say if it's really — warm at noon —
Whether it's Buttercups — that "skim" —
Or Butterflies — that "bloom"?
Then — skip — the frost — upon the lea —
And skip the Russet — on the tree —
Let's play those — never come!

It can't be "Summer"!
That — got through!
It's early — yet — for "Spring"!
There's that long town of White — to cross —
Before the Blackbirds sing!
It can't be "Dying"!
It's too Rouge —
The Dead shall go in White —
So Sunset shuts my question down
With Cuffs of Chrysolite!

Wild Nights — Wild Nights!
Were I with thee
Wild Nights should be
Our luxury!

Futile — the Winds —
To a Heart in port —
Done with the Compass —
Done with the Chart!

Rowing in Eden —
Ah, the Sea!
Might I but moor — Tonight —
In Thee!

Over the fence —
Strawberries — grow —
Over the fence —
I could climb — if I tried, I know —
Berries are nice!

But — if I stained my Apron —
God would certainly scold!
Oh, dear, — I guess if He were a Boy —
He'd — climb — if He could!

Of all the Souls that stand create —
I have elected — One —
When Sense from Spirit — files away —
And Subterfuge — is done —
When that which is — and that which was —
Apart — intrinsic — stand —
And this brief Drama in the flesh —
Is shifted — like a Sand —
When Figures show their royal Front —
And Mists — are carved away,
Behold the Atom — I preferred —
To all the lists of Clay!

What if I say I shall not wait!
What if I burst the fleshly Gate —
And pass escaped — to thee!

What if I file this Mortal — off —
See where it hurt me — That's enough —
And wade in Liberty!

They cannot take me — any more!
Dungeons can call — and Guns implore
Unmeaning — now — to me —

As laughter — was — an hour ago —
Or Laces — or a Travelling Show —
Or who died — yesterday!

A solemn thing — it was — I said —
A woman — white — to be —
And wear — if God should count me fit —
Her blameless mystery —

A hallowed thing — to drop a life
Into the purple well —
Too plummetless — that it return —
Eternity — until —

I pondered how the bliss would look —
And would it feel as big —
When I could take it in my hand —
As hovering — seen — through fog —

And then — the size of this "small" life —
The Sages — call it small —
Swelled — like Horizons — in my vest —
And I sneered — softly — "small"!

"Heaven" — is what I cannot reach!
The Apple on the Tree —
Provided it do hopeless —hang —
That — "Heaven" is — to Me!

The Color, on the Cruising Cloud —
The interdicted Land —
Behind the Hill — the House behind —
There — Paradise — is found!

Her teasing Purples — Afternoons —
The credulous — decoy —
Enamored — of the Conjuror —
That spurned us — Yesterday!

"Hope" is the thing with feathers —
That perches in the soul —
And sings the tune without the words —
And never stops — at all —

And sweetest — in the Gale — is heard —
And sore must be the storm —
That could abash the little Bird
That kept so many warm —

I've heard it in the chillest land —
And on the strangest Sea —
Yet, never, in Extremity,
It asked a crumb — of Me.

I'm nobody! Who are you?
Are you nobody, too?
Then there's a pair of us!
Don't tell! They'd banish us, you know.
How dreary to be somebody!
How public — like a frog
To tell your name — the livelong day
To an admiring Bog!

I felt a Funeral, in my Brain,
And Mourners to and fro
Kept reading — treading — till it seemed
That Sense was breaking through —

And when they all were seated,
A Service, like a Drum —
Kept beating — beating — till I thought
My mind was going numb —

And then I heard them lift a Box
And creak across my Soul
With those same Boots of Lead, again,
Then Space — began to toll

As all the Heavens were a Bell,
And Being, but an Ear,
And I, and Silence, some strange Race,
Wrecked, solitary, here —

And then a Plank in Reason, broke,
And I dropped down, and down —
And hit a World, at every plunge,
And Finished knowing — then —

I would not paint — a picture —
I'd rather be the One
Its bright impossibility
To dwell — delicious — on —
And wonder how the fingers feel
Whose rare — celestial — stir —
Evokes so sweet a Torment —
Such sumptuous — Despair —

I would not talk, like Cornets —
I'd rather be the One
Raised softly to the Ceilings —
And out, and easy on —
Through Villages of Ether —
Myself endued Balloon
By but a lip of Metal —
The pier to my Pontoon —

Nor would I be a Poet —
It's finer — own the Ear —
Enamored — impotent — content —
The License to revere,
A privilege so awful
What would the Dower be,
Had I the Art to stun myself
With Bolts of Melody!

If anybody's friend be dead
It's sharpest of the theme
The thinking how they walked alive —
At such and such a time —

Their costume, of a Sunday,
Some manner of the Hair —
A prank nobody knew but them
Lost, in the Sepulchre —

How warm, they were, on such a day,
You almost feel the date —
So short way off it seems —
And now — they're Centuries from that —

How pleased they were, at what you said —
You try to touch the smile
And dip your fingers in the frost —
When was it — Can you tell —

You asked the Company to tea —
Acquaintance — just a few —
And chatted close with this Grand Thing
That don't remember you —

Past Bows, and Invitations —
Past Interview, and Vow —
Past what Ourself can estimate —
That — makes the Quick of Woe!

A Bird came down the Walk,
He did not know I saw;
He bit an Angle Worm in halves
And ate the fellow, raw.

And then, he drank a dew
From a convenient Grass,
And then hopped sidewise to the
  Wall
To let a Beetle pass.

He glanced with rapid eyes
That hurried all abroad —
They looked like frightened beads,
  I thought
He stirred his velvet head

Like one in danger, Cautious,
I offered him a Crumb
And he unrolled his feathers
and rowed him softer home —

Than Oars divide the Ocean,
Too silver for a seam,
Or Butterflies, off Banks of Noon
Leap, plashless, as they swim.

I know a place where Summer strives
With such a practised Frost —
She — each year — leads her Daisies back
—

Recording briefly — "Lost" —

But when the South Wind stirs the Pools
And struggles in the lanes —
Her Heart misgives Her, for Her Vow —
And she pours soft Refrains

Into the lap of Adamant —
And spices — and the Dew —
That stiffens quietly to Quartz —
Upon her Amber Shoe —

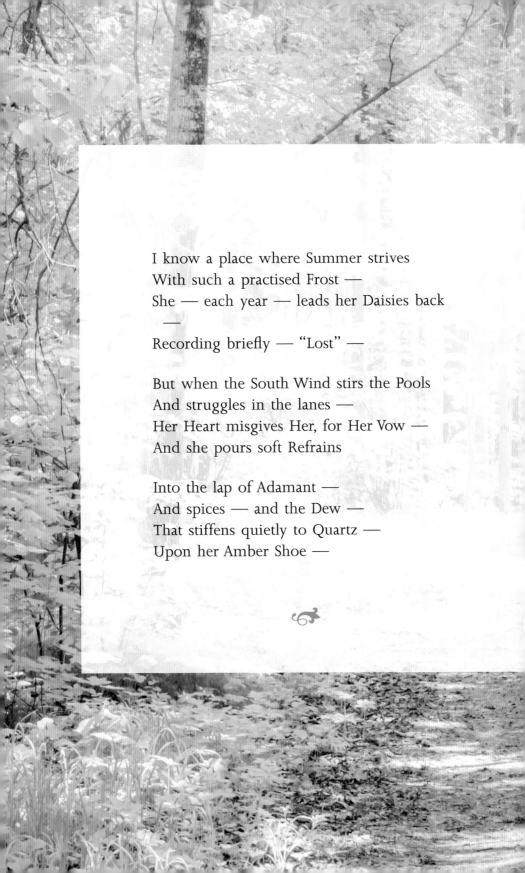

This World is not Conclusion.
A Species stands beyond —
Invisible, as Music —
But positive, as Sound —
It beckons, and it baffles —
Philosophy, don't know —
And through a Riddle, at the last —
Sagacity, must go —
To guess it, puzzles scholars —
To gain it, Men have borne
Contempt of Generations
And Crucifixion, shown —
Faith slips — and laughs, and rallies —
Blushes, if any see —
And asks a Vane, the way —
Much Gesture, from the Pulpit —
Strong Hallelujahs roll —
Narcotics cannot still the Tooth
That nibbles at the soul —

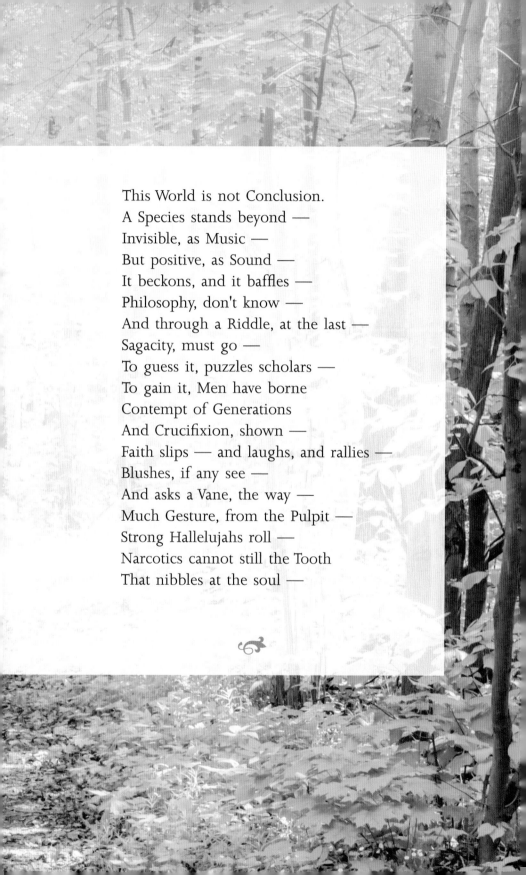

I envy Seas, whereon He rides —
I envy Spokes of Wheels
Of Chariots, that Him convey —
I envy Crooked Hills

That gaze upon His journey —
How easy All can see
What is forbidden utterly
As Heaven — unto me!

I envy Nests of Sparrows —
That dot His distant Eaves —
The wealthy Fly, upon His Pane —
The happy — happy Leaves —

That just abroad His Window
Have Summer's leave to play —
The Ear Rings of Pizarro
Could not obtain for me —

I envy Light — that wakes Him —
And Bells — that boldly ring
To tell Him it is Noon, abroad —
Myself — be Noon to Him —

Yet interdict — my Blossom —
And abrogate — my Bee —
Lest Noon in Everlasting Night —
Drop Gabriel — and Me —

Good Morning — Midnight —
I'm coming Home —
Day — got tired of Me —
How could I — of Him?

Sunshine was a sweet place —
I liked to stay —
But Morn — didn't want me — now —
So — Goodnight — Day!

I can look — can't I —
When the East is Red?
The Hills — have a way — then —
That puts the Heart — abroad —

You — are not so fair — Midnight —
I chose — Day —
But — please take a little Girl —
He turned away!

The Moon is distant from the Sea —
And yet, with Amber Hands —
She leads Him — docile as a Boy —
Along appointed Sands —

He never misses a Degree —
Obedient to Her Eye
He comes just so far — toward the Town —
Just so far — goes away —

Oh, Signor, Thine, the Amber Hand —
And mine — the distant Sea —
Obedient to the least command
Thine eye impose on me —

To hear an Oriole sing
May be a common thing —
Or only a divine.

It is not of the Bird
Who sings the same, unheard,
As unto Crowd —

The Fashion of the Ear
Attireth that it hear
In Dun, or fair —

So whether it be Rune,
Or whether it be none
Is of within.

The "Tune is in the Tree —"
The Skeptic — showeth me —
"No Sir! In Thee!"

I Years had been from Home
And now before the Door
I dared not enter, lest a Face
I never saw before

Stare solid into mine
And ask my Business there —
"My Business but a Life I left
Was such remaining there?"

I leaned upon the Awe —
I lingered with Before —
The Second like an Ocean rolled
And broke against my ear —

I laughed a crumbling Laugh
That I could fear a Door
Who Consternation compassed
And never winced before.

I fitted to the Latch
My Hand, with trembling care
Lest back the awful Door should spring
And leave me in the Floor —

Then moved my Fingers off
As cautiously as Glass
And held my ears, and like a Thief
Fled gasping from the House —

I died for beauty, but was scarce
Adjusted in the tomb,
When one who died for truth was lain
In an adjoining room.

He questioned softly "why I failed"?
"For beauty," I replied.
"And I for truth — the two are one —
We brethren are," he said.

And so, as kinsmen met a night,
We talked between the Rooms,
Until the moss had reached our lips,
And covered up our names.

She dealt her pretty words like Blades —
How glittering they shone —
And every One unbared a Nerve
Or wantoned with a Bone —

She never deemed — she hurt —
That — is not Steel's Affair —
A vulgar grimace in the Flesh —
How ill the Creatures bear —

To Ache is human — not polite —
The Film upon the eye
Mortality's old Custom —
Just locking up — to Die.

"Why do I love" You, Sir?
Because —
The Wind does not require the Grass
To answer — Wherefore when He pass
She cannot keep Her place.

Because He knows — and
Do not You —
And We know not —
Enough for Us
The Wisdom it be so —

The Lightning — never asked an Eye
Wherefore it shut — when He was by —
Because He knows it cannot speak —
And reasons not contained —
— Of Talk —
There be — preferred by Daintier Folk —

The Sunrise — Sir — compelleth Me —
Because He's Sunrise — and I see —
Therefore — Then —
I love Thee —

I dwell in Possibility —
A fairer House than Prose —
More numerous of Windows —
Superior — for Doors —

Of Chambers as the Cedars —
Impregnable of Eye —
And for an Everlasting Roof
The Gambrels of the Sky —

Of Visitors — the fairest —
For Occupation — This —
The spreading wide my narrow Hands
To gather Paradise —

Because I could not stop for Death —
He kindly stopped for me —
The Carriage held but just Ourselves —
And Immortality.

We slowly drove — He knew no haste,
And I had put away
My labor and my leisure too,
For His Civility —

We passed the School, where Children strove
At Recess — in the Ring —
We passed the Fields of Gazing Grain —
We passed the Setting Sun —

Or rather — He passed Us —
The Dews drew quivering and chill —
For only Gossamer, my Gown —
My Tippet — only Tulle —

We paused before a House that seemed
A Swelling of the Ground —
The Roof was scarcely visible —
The Cornice — in the Ground —

Since then — 'tis centuries — and yet
Feels shorter than the Day
I first surmised the Horses' Heads
Were toward Eternity —

The Wind didn't come from the Orchard —
  today —
Further than that —
Nor stop to play with the Hay —
Nor joggle a Hat —
He's a transitive fellow — very —
Rely on that —

If He leave a Bur at the door
We know He has climbed a Fir —
But the Fir is Where — Declare —
Were you ever there?

If He brings Odors of Clovers —
And that is His business — not Ours —
Then He has been with the Mowers —
Whetting away the Hours
To sweet pauses of Hay —
His Way — of a June Day —

If He fling Sand, and Pebble —
Little Boys Hats — and Stubble —
With an occasional Steeple —
And a hoarse "Get out of the way, I say,"
Who'd be the fool to stay?
Would you — Say —
Would you be the fool to stay?

The Spider holds a Silver Ball
In unperceived Hands —
And dancing softly to Himself
His Yarn of Pearl — unwinds —

He plies from Nought to Nought —
In unsubstantial Trade —
Supplants our Tapestries with His —
In half the period —

An Hour to rear supreme
His Continents of Light —
Then dangle from the Housewife's Broom —
His Boundaries — forgot —

This is my letter to the World
That never wrote to Me —
The simple News that Nature told —
With tender Majesty

Her Message is committed
To Hands I cannot see —
For love of Her — Sweet — countrymen —
Judge tenderly — of Me

We learned the Whole of Love —
The Alphabet — the Words —
A Chapter — then the mighty Book —
Then — Revelation closed —

But in Each Other's eyes
An Ignorance beheld —
Diviner than the Childhood's —
And each to each, a Child —

Attempted to expound
What Neither — understood —
Alas, that Wisdom is so large —
And Truth — so manifold!

The Test of Love — is Death —
Our Lord — "so loved" — it saith —
What Largest Lover — hath
Another — doth —

If smaller Patience — be —
Through less Infinity —
If Bravo, sometimes swerve —
Through fainter Nerve —

Accept its Most —
And overlook — the Dust —
Last — Least —
The Cross' — Request —

The Black Berry — wears a Thorn in his side —
But no Man heard Him cry —
He offers His Berry, just the same
To Partridge — and to Boy —

He sometimes holds upon the Fence —
Or struggles to a Tree —
Or clasps a Rock, with both His Hands —
But not for Sympathy —

We — tell a Hurt — to cool it —
This Mourner — to the Sky
A little further reaches — instead —
Brave Black Berry —

I measure every Grief I meet
With narrow, probing, Eyes —
I wonder if It weighs like Mine —
Or has an Easier size.

I wonder if They bore it long —
Or did it just begin —
I could not tell the Date of Mine —
It feels so old a pain —

I wonder if it hurts to live —
And if They have to try —
And whether — could They choose between —
It would not be — to die —

I note that Some — gone patient long —
At length, renew their smile —
An imitation of a Light
That has so little Oil —

I wonder if when Years have piled —
Some Thousands — on the Harm —
That hurt them early — such a lapse
Could give them any Balm —

Or would they go on aching still
Through Centuries of Nerve —
Enlightened to a larger Pain —
In Contrast with the Love —

The Grieved — are many — I am told —
There is the various Cause —
Death — is but one — and comes but once —
And only nails the eyes —

There's Grief of Want — and Grief of Cold —
A sort they call "Despair" —
There's Banishment from native Eyes —
In sight of Native Air —

And though I may not guess the kind —
Correctly — yet to me
A piercing Comfort it affords
In passing Calvary —

To note the fashions — of the Cross —
And how they're mostly worn —
Still fascinated to presume
That Some — are like My Own —

Two butterflies went out at Noon —
And waltzed upon a Farm —
Then stepped straight through the Firmament
And rested, on a Beam —

And then — together bore away
Upon a shining Sea —
Though never yet, in any Port —
Their coming, mentioned — be —

If spoken by the distant Bird —
If met in Ether Sea
By Frigate, or by Merchantman —
No notice — was — to me —

The Angle of a Landscape —
That every time I wake —
Between my Curtain and the Wall
Upon an ample Crack —

Like a Venetian — waiting —
Accosts my open eye —
Is just a Bough of Apples —
Held slanting, in the Sky —

The Pattern of a Chimney —
The Forehead of a Hill —
Sometimes — a Vane's Forefinger —
But that's — Occasional —

The Seasons — shift — my Picture —
Upon my Emerald Bough,
I wake — to find no — Emeralds —
Then — Diamonds — which the Snow

From Polar Caskets — fetched me —
The Chimney — and the Hill —
And just the Steeple's finger —
These — never stir at all —

The heart asks Pleasure first.
And then, excuse from pain —
And then, those little Anodynes
That deaden suffering

And then, to go to sleep;
And then, if it should be
The will of its Inquisitor
The liberty to die.

I heard a Fly buzz — when I died —
The Stillness in the Room
Was like the Stillness in the Air —
Between the Heaves of Storm —

The Eyes around — had wrung them dry —
And Breaths were gathering firm
For that last Onset — when the King
Be witnessed — in the Room —

I willed my Keepsakes — Signed away
What portion of me be
Assignable — and then it was
There interposed a Fly —

With Blues — uncertain stumbling Buzz —
Between the light — and me —
And then the Windows failed — and then
I could not see to see —

You cannot put a Fire out —
A Thing that can ignite
Can go, itself, without a Fan —
Upon the slowest Night —

You cannot fold a Flood —
And put it in a Drawer —
Because the Winds would find it out —
And tell your Cedar Floor —

The Night was wide, and furnished scant
With but a single Star —
That often as a Cloud it met —
Blew out itself — for fear —

The Wind pursued the little Bush —
And drove away the Leaves
November left — then clambered up
And fretted in the Eaves —

No Squirrel went abroad —
A Dog's belated feet
Like intermittent Plush, he heard
Adown the empty Street —

To feel if Blinds be fast —
And closer to the fire —
Her little Rocking Chair to draw —
And shiver for the Poor —

The Housewife's gentle Task —
How pleasanter — said she
Unto the Sofa opposite —
The Sleet — than May, no Thee —

Much Madness is divinest Sense —
To a discerning Eye —
Much sense — the starkest madness —
'Tis the Majority
In this, as All, prevails.
Assent — and you are sane —
Demur, — you're straightway dangerous —
And handled with a Chain —

The Wind — tapped like a tired Man —
And like a Host — "Come in"
I boldly answered — entered then
My Residence within

A Rapid — footless Guest —
To offer whom a Chair
Were as impossible as hand
A Sofa to the Air —

No Bone had He to bind Him —
His Speech was like the Push
Of numerous Humming Birds at once
From a superior Bush —

His Countenance — a Billow —
His Fingers, as He passed
Let go a music — as of tunes
Blown tremulous in Glass —

He visited — still flitting —
Then like a timid Man
Again, He tapped — 'twas flurriedly —
And I became alone —

Sweet — You forgot — but I remembered
Every time — for Two —
So that the Sum be never hindered
Through Decay of You —

Say if I erred? Accuse my Farthings —
Blame the little Hand
Happy it be for You — a Beggar's —
Seeking More — to spend —

Just to be Rich — to waste my Guineas
On so Best a Heart —
Just to be Poor — for Barefoot Vision
You — Sweet — Shut me out —

I could not prove the Years had feet —
Yet confident they run
Am I, from symptoms that are past
And Series that are done —

I find my feet have further Goals —
I smile upon the Aims
That felt so ample — Yesterday —
Today's — have vaster claims —

I do not doubt the self I was
Was competent to me —
But something awkward in the fit —
Proves that — outgrown — I see —

Funny — to be a Century —
And see the People — going by —
I — should die of the Oddity —
But then — I'm not so staid — as He —

He keeps His Secrets safely — very —
Were He to tell — extremely sorry
This Bashful Globe of Ours would be —
So dainty of Publicity —

Don't put up my Thread and Needle —
I'll begin to Sew
When the Birds begin to whistle —
Better Stitches — so —

These were bent — my sight got crooked —
When my mind — is plain
I'll do seams — a Queen's endeavor
Would not blush to own —

Hems — too fine for Lady's tracing
To the sightless Knot —
Tucks — of dainty interspersion —
Like a dotted Dot —

Leave my Needle in the furrow —
Where I put it down —
I can make the zigzag stitches
Straight — when I am strong —

Till then — dreaming I am sewing
Fetch the seam I missed —
Closer — so I — at my sleeping —
Still surmise I stitch —

Forever — is composed of Nows —
'Tis not a different time —
Except for Infiniteness —
And Latitude of Home —

From this — experienced Here —
Remove the Dates — to These —
Let Months dissolve in further Months —
And Years — exhale in Years —

Without Debate — or Pause —
Or Celebrated Days —
No different Our Years would be
From Anno Domini's —

The power to be true to You,
Until upon my face
The Judgment push his Picture —
Presumptuous of Your Place —

Of This — Could Man deprive Me —
Himself — the Heaven excel —
Whose invitation — Yours reduced
Until it showed too small —

Doom is the House without the Door —
'Tis entered from the Sun —
And then the Ladder's thrown away,
Because Escape — is done —

'Tis varied by the Dream
Of what they do outside —
Where Squirrels play — and Berries die —
And Hemlocks — bow — to God —

The Sun kept setting — setting — still
No Hue of Afternoon —
Upon the Village I perceived
From House to House 'twas Noon —

The Dusk kept dropping — dropping — still
No Dew upon the Grass —
But only on my Forehead stopped —
And wandered in my Face —

My Feet kept drowsing — drowsing — still
My fingers were awake —
Yet why so little sound — Myself
Unto my Seeming — make?

How well I knew the Light before —
I could see it now —
'Tis Dying — I am doing — but
I'm not afraid to know —

A Thought went up my mind today —
That I have had before —
But did not finish — some way back —
I could not fix the Year —

Nor where it went — nor why it came
The second time to me —
Nor definitely, what it was —
Have I the Art to say —

But somewhere — in my Soul — I know —
I've met the Thing before —
It just reminded me — 'twas all —
And came my way no more —

Nature — the Gentlest Mother is,
Impatient of no Child —
The feeblest — or the waywardest —
Her Admonition mild —

In Forest — and the Hill —
By Traveller — be heard —
Restraining Rampant Squirrel —
Or too impetuous Bird —

How fair Her Conversation —
A Summer Afternoon —
Her Household — Her Assembly —
And when the Sun go down —

Her Voice among the Aisles
Incite the timid prayer
Of the minutest Cricket —
The most unworthy Flower —

When all the Children sleep —
She turns as long away
As will suffice to light Her lamps —
Then bending from the Sky —

With infinite Affection —
And infiniter Care —
Her Golden finger on Her lip —
Wills Silence — Everywhere —

Sweet Mountains — Ye tell Me no lie —
Never deny Me — Never fly —
Those same unvarying Eyes
Turn on Me — when I fail — or feign,
Or take the Royal names in vain —
Their far — slow — Violet Gaze —

My Strong Madonnas — Cherish still —
The Wayward Nun — beneath the Hill —
Whose service — is to You —
Her latest Worship — When the Day
Fades from the Firmament away —
To lift Her Brows on You —

Where Thou art — that — is Home —
Cashmere — or Calvary — the same —
Degree — or Shame —
I scarce esteem Location's Name —
So I may Come —

What Thou dost — is Delight —
Bondage as Play — be sweet —
Imprisonment — Content —
And Sentence — Sacrament —
Just We two — meet —

Where Thou art not — is Woe —
Tho' Bands of Spices — row —
What Thou dost not — Despair —
Tho' Gabriel — praise me — Sir —

Grief is a Mouse —
And chooses Wainscot in the Breast
For His Shy House —
And baffles quest —

Grief is a Thief — quick startled —
Pricks His Ear — report to hear
Of that Vast Dark —
That swept His Being — back —

Grief is a Juggler — boldest at the Play —
Lest if He flinch — the eye that way
Pounce on His Bruises — One — say — or
   Three —
Grief is a Gourmand — spare His luxury —

Best Grief is Tongueless — before He'll tell —
Burn Him in the Public Square —
His Ashes — will
Possibly — if they refuse — How then know
   —
Since a Rack couldn't coax a syllable — now.

I had no time to Hate —
Because
The Grave would hinder Me —
And Life was not so
Ample I
Could finish — Enmity —

Nor had I time to Love —
But since
Some Industry must be —
The little Toil of Love —
I thought
Be large enough for Me —

My Life had stood — a Loaded Gun —
In Corners — till a Day
The Owner passed — identified —
And carried Me away —

And now We roam in Sovereign Woods —
And now We hunt the Doe —
And every time I speak for Him —
The Mountains straight reply —

And do I smile, such cordial light
Upon the Valley glow —
It is as a Vesuvian face
Had let its pleasure through —

And when at Night — Our good Day done —
I guard My Master's Head —
'Tis better than the Eider-Duck's
Deep Pillow — to have shared —

To foe of His — I'm deadly foe —
None stir the second time —
On whom I lay a Yellow Eye —
Or an emphatic Thumb —

Though I than He — may longer live
He longer must — than I —
For I have but the power to kill,
Without — the power to die —

Never for Society
He shall seek in vain —
Who His own acquaintance
Cultivate — Of Men
Wiser Men may weary —
But the Man within

Never knew Satiety —
Better entertain
Than could Border Ballad —
Or Biscayan Hymn —
Neither introduction
Need You — unto Him —

The Wind begun to knead the Grass —
As Women do a Dough —
He flung a Hand full at the Plain —
A Hand full at the Sky —
The Leaves unhooked themselves from Trees
—
And started all abroad —
The Dust did scoop itself like Hands —
And throw away the Road —
The Wagons — quickened on the Street —
The Thunders gossiped low —
The Lightning showed a Yellow Head —
And then a livid Toe —
The Birds put up the Bars to Nests —
The Cattle flung to Barns —
Then came one drop of Giant Rain —
And then, as if the Hands
That held the Dams — had parted hold —
The Waters Wrecked the Sky —
But overlooked my Father's House —
Just Quartering a Tree —

As Sleigh Bells seem in summer
Or Bees, at Christmas show —
So fairy — so fictitious
The individuals do
Repealed from observation —
A Party that we knew —
More distant in an instant
Than Dawn in Timbuctoo.

These Strangers, in a foreign World,
Protection asked of me —
Befriend them, lest Yourself in Heaven
Be found a Refugee —

The Robin for the Crumb
Returns no syllable
But long records the Lady's name
In Silver Chronicle.

This Consciousness that is aware
Of Neighbors and the Sun
Will be the one aware of Death
And that itself alone

Is traversing the interval
Experience between
And most profound experiment
Appointed unto Men —

How adequate unto itself
Its properties shall be
Itself unto itself and none
Shall make discovery —

Adventure most unto itself
The Soul condemned to be —
Attended by a single Hound
Its own identity.

A Drop Fell on the Apple Tree —
Another — on the Roof —
A Half a Dozen kissed the Eaves —
And made the Gables laugh —

A few went out to help the Brook
That went to help the Sea —
Myself Conjectured were they Pearls —
What Necklaces could be —

The Dust replaced, in Hoisted Roads —
The Birds jocoser sung —
The Sunshine threw his Hat away —
The Bushes — spangles flung —

The Breezes brought dejected Lutes —
And bathed them in the Glee —
Then Orient showed a single Flag,
And signed the Fete away —

She staked her Feathers — Gained an Arc —
Debated — Rose again —
This time — beyond the estimate
Of Envy, or of Men —

And now, among Circumference —
Her steady Boat be seen —
At home — among the Billows — As
The Bough where she was born —

Time feels so vast that were it not
For an Eternity —
I fear me this Circumference
Engross my Finity —

To His exclusion, who prepare
By Processes of Size
For the Stupendous Vision
Of his diameters —

Expectation — is Contentment —
Gain — Satiety —
But Satiety — Conviction
Of Necessity

Of an Austere trait in Pleasure —
Good, without alarm
Is a too established Fortune —
Danger — deepens Sum —

I felt a Cleaving in my Mind —
As if my Brain had split —
I tried to match it — Seam by Seam —
But could not make them fit.

The thought behind, I strove to join
Unto the thought before —
But Sequence ravelled out of Sound
Like Balls — upon a Floor.

Further in Summer than the Birds —
Pathetic from the Grass —
A Minor Nation celebrates
Its unobtrusive Mass —

No Ordinance be seen —
So gradual the Grace
A pensive Custom it becomes
Enlarging Loneliness —

'Tis Audiblest, at Dusk —
When Day's attempt is done —
And Nature nothing waits to do
But terminate in Tune —

Nor difference it knows
Of Cadence, or of Pause —
But simultaneous as Same —
The Service emphasize —

Nor know I when it cease —
At Candles, it is here —
When Sunrise is — that it is not —
Than this, I know no more —

The Earth has many keys —
Where Melody is not
Is the Unknown Peninsula —
Beauty — is Nature's Fact —

But Witness for Her Land —
And Witness for Her Sea —
The Cricket is Her utmost
Of Elegy, to Me —

Finding is the first Act
The second, loss,
Third, Expedition for
The "Golden Fleece"

Fourth, no Discovery—
Fifth, no Crew—
Finally, no Golden Fleece —
Jason — sham — too.

As Frost is best conceived
By force of its Result —
Affliction is inferred
By subsequent effect —

If when the sun reveal,
The Garden keep the Gash —
If as the Days resume
The wilted countenance

Cannot correct the crease
Or counteract the stain —
Presumption is Vitality
Was somewhere put in twain.

The Poets light but Lamps —
Themselves — go out —
The Wicks they stimulate —
If vital Light

Inhere as do the Suns —
Each Age a Lens
Disseminating their
Circumference —

I made slow Riches but my Gain
Was steady as the Sun
And every Night, it numbered more
Than the preceding One

All Days, I did not earn the same
But my perceiveless Gain
Inferred the less by Growing than
The Sum that it had grown.

A Light exists in Spring
Not present on the Year
At any other period —
When March is scarcely here

A Color stands abroad
On Solitary Fields
That Science cannot overtake
But Human Nature feels.

It waits upon the Lawn,
It shows the furthest Tree
Upon the furthest Slope you know
It almost speaks to you.

Then as Horizons step
Or Noons report away
Without the Formula of sound
It passes and we stay —

A quality of loss
Affecting our Content
As Trade had suddenly encroached
Upon a Sacrament.

How far is it to Heaven?
As far as Death this way —
Of River or of Ridge beyond
Was no discovery.

How far is it to Hell?
As far as Death this way —
How far left hand the Sepulchre
Defies Topography.

Two Travellers perishing in Snow
The Forests as they froze
Together heard them strengthening
Each other with the words

That Heaven if Heaven — must contain
What Either left behind
And then the cheer too solemn grew
For language, and the wind

Long steps across the features took
That Love had touched the Morn
With reverential Hyacinth —
The taleless Days went on

Till Mystery impatient drew
And those They left behind
Led absent, were procured of Heaven
As Those first furnished, said —

Peace is a fiction of our Faith —
The Bells a Winter Night
Bearing the Neighbor out of Sound
That never did alight.

If I can stop one Heart from breaking,
I shall not live in vain
If I can ease one Life the Aching,
Or cool one Pain

Or help one fainting Robin
Unto his Nest again
I shall not live in Vain.

Three Weeks passed since I had seen Her —
Some Disease had vext
'Twas with Text and Village Singing
I beheld Her next

And a Company — our pleasure
To discourse alone —
Gracious now to me as any —
Gracious unto none —

Borne without dissent of Either
To the Parish night —
Of the Separated Parties
Which be out of sight?

Crumbling is not an instant's Act
A fundamental pause
Dilapidation's processes
Are organized Decays.

'Tis first a Cobweb on the Soul
A Cuticle of Dust
A Borer in the Axis
An Elemental Rust —

Ruin is formal — Devil's work
Consecutive and slow —
Fail in an instant, no man did
Slipping — is Crash's law.

This Chasm, Sweet, upon my life
I mention it to you,
When Sunrise through a fissure drop
The Day must follow too.

If we demur, its gaping sides
Disclose as 'twere a Tomb
Ourself am lying straight wherein
The Favorite of Doom.

When it has just contained a Life
Then, Darling, it will close
And yet so bolder every Day
So turbulent it grows

I'm tempted half to stitch it up
With a remaining Breath
I should not miss in yielding, though
To Him, it would be Death —

And so I bear it big about
My Burial — before
A Life quite ready to depart
Can harass me no more —

The Sun and Moon must make their haste —
The Stars express around
For in the Zones of Paradise
The Lord alone is burned —

His Eye, it is the East and West —
The North and South when He
Do concentrate His Countenance
Like Glow Worms, flee away —

Oh Poor and Far —
Oh Hindred Eye
That hunted for the Day —
The Lord a Candle entertains
Entirely for Thee —

How happy I was if I could forget
To remember how sad I am
Would be an easy adversity
But the recollecting of Bloom

Keeps making November difficult
Till I who was almost bold
Lose my way like a little Child
And perish of the cold.

A narrow fellow in the grass
Occasionally rides;
You may have met him — did you not
His notice instant is,
The grass divides as with a comb,
A spotted shaft is seen,
And then it closes at your feet,
And opens further on.

He likes a boggy acre
A floor too cool for corn,
Yet when a boy and barefoot,
I more than once at noon
Have passed, I thought, a whip lash,
Unbraiding in the sun,

When stooping to secure it,
It wrinkled and was gone.

Several of nature's people
I know, and they know me;
I feel for them a transport
Of cordiality.
Yet never met this fellow,
Attended or alone,
Without a tighter breathing,
And zero at the bone.

This is a Blossom of the Brain —
A small — italic Seed
Lodged by Design or Happening
The Spirit fructified —

Shy as the Wind of his Chambers
Swift as a Freshet's Tongue
So of the Flower of the Soul
Its process is unknown.

When it is found, a few rejoice
The Wise convey it Home
Carefully cherishing the spot
If other Flower become.

When it is lost, that Day shall be
The Funeral of God,
Upon his Breast, a closing Soul
The Flower of our Lord.

Gratitude — is not the mention
Of a Tenderness,
But its still appreciation
Out of Plum of Speech.

When the Sea return no Answer
By the Line and Lead
Prove it there's no Sea, or rather
A remoter Bed?

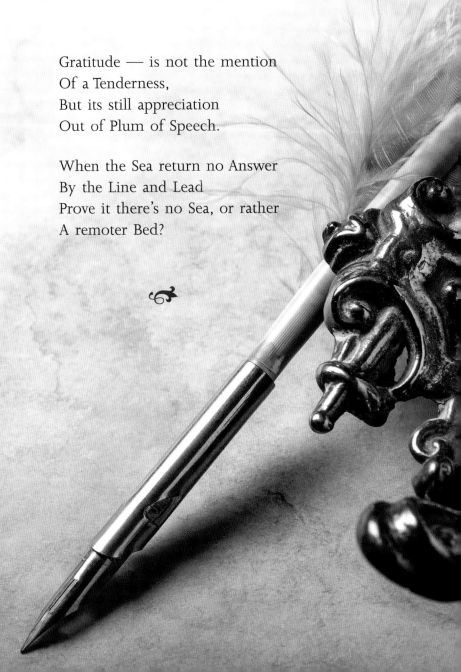

The Frost of Death was on the Pane —
"Secure your Flower" said he.
Like Sailors fighting with a Leak
We fought Mortality.

Our passive Flower we held to Sea —
To Mountain — To the Sun —
Yet even on his Scarlet shelf
To crawl the Frost begun —

We pried him back
Ourselves we wedged
Himself and her between,
Yet easy as the narrow Snake
He forked his way along

Till all her helpless beauty bent
And then our wrath begun —
We hunted him to his Ravine
We chased him to his Den —

We hated Death and hated Life
And nowhere was to go —
Than Sea and continent there is
A larger — it is Woe —

These are the Nights that Beetles love —
From Eminence remote
Drives ponderous perpendicular
His figure intimate
The terror of the Children
The merriment of men
Depositing his Thunder
He hoists abroad again —
A Bomb upon the Ceiling
Is an improving thing —
It keeps the nerves progressive
Conjecture flourishing —
Too dear the Summer evening
Without discreet alarm —
Supplied by Entomology
With its remaining charm —

The Snow that never drifts —
The transient, fragrant snow
That comes a single time a Year
Is softly driving now —

So thorough in the Tree
At night beneath the star
That it was February's Foot
Experience would swear —

Like Winter as a Face
We stern and former knew
Repaired of all but Loneliness
By Nature's Alibi —

Were every storm so spice
The Value could not be —
We buy with contrast — Pang is good
As near as memory —

The duties of the Wind are few,
To cast the ships, at Sea,
Establish March, the Floods escort,
And usher Liberty.

The pleasures of the Wind are broad,
To dwell Extent among,
Remain, or wander,
Speculate, or Forests entertain.

The kinsmen of the Wind are Peaks
Azof — the Equinox,
Also with Bird and Asteroid
A bowing intercourse.

The limitations of the Wind
Do he exist, or die,
Too wise he seems for Wakelessness,
However, know not I.

So much of Heaven has gone from Earth
That there must be a Heaven
If only to enclose the Saints
To Affidavit given.

The Missionary to the Mole
Must prove there is a Sky
Location doubtless he would plead
But what excuse have I?

Too much of Proof affronts Belief
The Turtle will not try
Unless you leave him — then return
And he has hauled away.

Tell all the Truth but tell it slant —
Success in Circuit lies
Too bright for our infirm Delight
The Truth's superb surprise

As Lightning to the Children eased
With explanation kind
The Truth must dazzle gradually
Or every man be blind —

There is no Frigate like a Book
To take us Lands away
Nor any Coursers like a Page
Of prancing Poetry —
This Traverse may the poorest take
Without opress of Toll —
How frugal is the Chariot
That bears the Human soul.

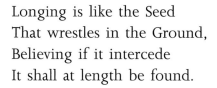

Longing is like the Seed
That wrestles in the Ground,
Believing if it intercede
It shall at length be found.

The Hour, and the Clime —
Each Circumstance unknown,
What Constancy must be achieved
Before it see the Sun!

As Summer into Autumn slips
And yet we sooner say
"The Summer" than "the Autumn," lest
We turn the sun away,

And almost count it an Affront
The presence to concede
Of one however lovely, not
The one that we have loved —

So we evade the charge of Years
On one attempting shy
The Circumvention of the Shaft
Of Life's Declivity.

Not with a Club, the Heart is broken
Nor with a Stone —
A Whip so small you could not see it
I've known

To lash the Magic Creature
Till it fell,
Yet that Whip's Name
Too noble then to tell.

Magnanimous as Bird
By Boy descried —
Singing unto the Stone
Of which it died —

Shame need not crouch
In such an Earth as Ours —
Shame — stand erect —
The Universe is yours.

❧

What mystery pervades a well!
That water lives so far —
A neighbor from another world
Residing in a jar

Whose limit none have ever seen,
But just his lid of glass —
Like looking every time you please
In an abyss's face!

The grass does not appear afraid,
I often wonder he
Can stand so close and look so bold
At what is awe to me.

Related somehow they may be,
The sedge stands next the sea —
Where he is floorless
And does no timidity betray

But nature is a stranger yet;
The ones that cite her most
Have never passed her haunted house,
Nor simplified her ghost.

To pity those that know her not
Is helped by the regret
That those who know her, know her less
The nearer her they get.

'Tis whiter than an Indian Pipe —
'Tis dimmer than a Lace —
No stature has it, like a Fog
When you approach the place —
Now any voice imply it here
Or intimate it there
A spirit — how doth it accost —
What function hath the Air?
This limitless Hyperbole
Each one of us shall be —
'Tis Drama — if Hypothesis
It be not Tragedy —

The fascinating chill that music leaves
Is Earth's corroboration
Of Ecstasy's impediment —
'Tis Rapture's germination
In timid and tumultuous soil
A fine — estranging creature —
To something upper wooing us
But not to our Creator —

You cannot make Remembrance grow
When it has lost its Root —
The tightening the Soil around
And setting it upright
Deceives perhaps the Universe
But not retrieves the Plant —
Real Memory, like Cedar Feet
Is shod with Adamant —
Nor can you cut Remembrance down
When it shall once have grown —
Its Iron Buds will sprout anew
However overthrown —

A faded Boy — in sallow Clothes
Who drove a lonesome Cow
To pastures of Oblivion —
A statesman's Embryo —

The Boys that whistled are extinct —
The Cows that fed and thanked
Remanded to a Ballad's Barn
Or Clover's Retrospect —

The Butterfly upon the Sky,
That doesn't know its Name
And hasn't any tax to pay
And hasn't any Home
Is just as high as you and I,
And higher, I believe,
So soar away and never sigh
And that's the way to grieve —

Those — dying then,
Knew where they went —
They went to God's Right Hand
  —
That Hand is amputated now
And God cannot be found —

The abdication of Belief
Makes the Behavior small —
Better an ignis fatuus
Than no illume at all —

No ladder needs the bird but skies
To situate its wings,
Nor any leader's grim baton
Arraigns it as it sings.
The implements of bliss are few —
As Jesus says of Him,
"Come unto me" the moiety
That wafts the cherubim.

There came a Wind like a Bugle —
It quivered through the Grass
And a Green Chill upon the Heat
So ominous did pass
We barred the Windows and the Doors
As from an Emerald Ghost —
The Doom's electric Moccasin
That very instant passed —
On a strange Mob of panting Trees
And Fences fled away
And Rivers where the Houses ran
Those looked that lived — that Day —
The Bell within the steeple wild
The flying tidings told —
How much can come
And much can go,
And yet abide the World!

The Spirit lasts — but in what mode —
Below, the Body speaks,
But as the Spirit furnishes —
Apart, it never talks —
The Music in the Violin
Does not emerge alone
But Arm in Arm with Touch, yet Touch
Alone — is not a Tune —
The Spirit lurks within the Flesh
Like Tides within the Sea
That make the Water live, estranged
What would the Either be?
Does that know — now — or does it cease —
That which to this is done,
Resuming at a mutual date
With every future one?
Instinct pursues the Adamant,
Exacting this Reply —
Adversity if it may be, or
Wild Prosperity,
The Rumor's Gate was shut so tight
Before my Mind was sown,
Not even a Prognostic's Push
Could make a Dent thereon —

⁊

A Drunkard cannot meet a Cork
Without a Revery —
And so encountering a Fly
This January Day
Jamaicas of Remembrance stir
That send me reeling in —
The moderate drinker of Delight
Does not deserve the spring —
Of juleps, part are in the Jug
And more are in the joy —
Your connoisseur in Liquours
Consults the Bumble Bee —

Not knowing when the Dawn will come,
I open every Door,
Or has it Feathers, like a Bird,
Or Billows, like a Shore —

Beauty crowds me till I die
Beauty mercy have on me
But if I expire today
Let it be in sight of thee —

There is a solitude of space
A solitude of sea
A solitude of death, but these
Society shall be
Compared with that profounder site
That polar privacy
A soul admitted to itself —
Finite infinity.

I did not reach Thee
But my feet slip nearer every day
Three Rivers and a Hill to cross
One Desert and a Sea
I shall not count the journey one
When I am telling thee.

Two deserts, but the Year is cold
So that will help the sand
One desert crossed —
The second one
Will feel as cool as land
Sahara is too little price
To pay for thy Right hand.

The Sea comes last — Step merry, feet,
So short we have to go —
To play together we are prone,
But we must labor now,
The last shall be the lightest load
That we have had to draw.

The Sun goes crooked —
That is Night
Before he makes the bend.
We must have passed the Middle Sea —
Almost we wish the End
Were further off —
Too great it seems
So near the Whole to stand.

We step like Plush,
We stand like snow,
The waters murmur new.
Three rivers and the Hill are passed —
Two deserts and the sea!
Now Death usurps my Premium
And gets the look at Thee.

Sometimes with the Heart
Seldom with the Soul
Scarcer once with the Might
Few — love at all.

Her face was in a bed of hair,
Like flowers in a plot —
Her hand was whiter than the sperm
That feeds the sacred light.
Her tongue more tender than the tune
That totters in the leaves —
Who hears may be incredulous,
Who witnesses, believes.

Love can do all but raise the Dead
I doubt if even that
From such a giant were withheld
Were flesh equivalent

But love is tired and must sleep,
And hungry and must graze
And so abets the shining Fleet
Till it is out of gaze.

Fame is a bee.
  It has a song —
It has a sting —
  Ah, too, it has a wing.

The saddest noise, the sweetest noise,
The maddest noise that grows, —
The birds, they make it in the spring,
At night's delicious close.

Between the March and April line —
That magical frontier
Beyond which summer hesitates,
Almost too heavenly near.

It makes us think of all the dead
That sauntered with us here,
By separation's sorcery
Made cruelly more dear.

It makes us think of what we had,
And what we now deplore.
We almost wish those siren throats
Would go and sing no more.

An ear can break a human heart
As quickly as a spear,
We wish the ear had not a heart
So dangerously near.

Index of First Lines